SMART

FOOTBALL OFFICIATING

How to Get Better Every Game

by Jeffrey Stern
Referee senior editor

Referee Enterprises, Inc., Franksville, Wis.

SMART FOOTBALL OFFICIATING:
HOW TO GET BETTER EVERY GAME
by Jeffrey Stern

Copyright © 2008 by Referee Enterprises, Inc.
P.O. Box 161, Franksville, Wis. 53126.
First printing 2002
Second printing 2007

Cover design by Matt Bowen

Printed in the United States of America

ISBN 1-58208-026-7

Tony Smith,
Illinois

Table of Contents

Introduction

Congratulations! Good job!

Those are words officials probably don't hear very often. But I think they are appropriate in this case.

By purchasing and reading this book, you have demonstrated a desire to improve your officiating. If you do indeed improve:

• You benefit, by earning more assignments at higher levels of play.

• The teams benefit, by having their games officiated properly.

• Young officials benefit, because you as a more experienced and skilled official can impart valuable advice and information to them.

I'd like to thank Jerry Grunska and George Demetriou, two men whose work is familiar to *Referee* readers, for contributing chapters to this book. In addition to providing some text, *Referee* Editor Bill Topp reviewed the book, co-wrote a chapter and provided valuable guidance. Matt Bowen and Carrie Kwasniewski of the creative department lent their considerable talent to the design and layout of the book.

The book you hold is the result of much effort and creativity. I hope you experience the same enlightenment I did. If you have some information, advice or experiences to share, I'd love to hear about them.

Thanks for your investment of time and money. I hope you think both were well-spent.

Jeffrey Stern
Referee senior editor

1

Some ABCs of Officiating

By Jeffrey Stern

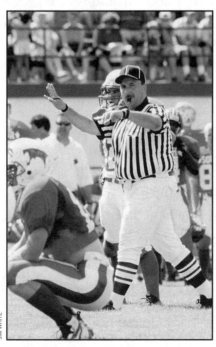

JIM WHITE

Dave Powers,
Indiana

The first chapter of any book is important. It sets the stage for what follows. In murder mysteries, the victim usually gets his goose cooked in the opening chapter. In do-it-yourself manuals, important safety tips often make up the first pages. In this book, I've chosen some basic tips, reminders and principles as the stage-setter.

Here's a breeze through the alphabet offering tips or considerations for every letter (including Q and X, which took some doing).

Awareness of game situations. Most football fans understand how the down, distance, score and time remaining affect how teams strategize. The same information that helps the guy in the 53rd row can help officials if they use a little common sense.

For example, it's third down and 11. Team A trails by two points with 1:37 to play in the fourth quarter and has the ball on its own 44 yardline. Going without a huddle because it is out of timeouts, team A lines up in a shotgun formation with three eligible receivers on the right side of the formation.

Gee, do you think a pass is coming?

Gee, do you think a pass is coming? Do you think the receivers will run at least 11-yard routes? Is it likely the quarterback's first look will be to a receiver running a pattern near the sideline?

That is a fairly elementary example, but it illustrates how officials can process information and turn it into proper coverage of a play.

The latter stages of a game are also prime times for flea-flickers or other trick plays, onside kicks, clock-killing spikes

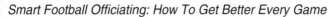

(and fake spikes) and other tactics that are less than routine. Your ability to anticipate them will help determine if you are in proper position to make a big call (or no-call) at the end of a game.

Good officials recognize when trouble between opponents is brewing. It doesn't always happen at the end of a one-sided game when the trailing team figures it has nothing to lose by resorting to cheap shots. Take care of those problems early and you may well prevent a full-scale brawl.

In a nutshell, successful officials not only look the part, act the part and have good judgment. The truly good ones never stop thinking and anticipating.

Good officials recognize when trouble between opponents is brewing.

Communication between officials should be by word and by signal. Every official should signal the down after every play. Officials with player-counting responsibilities must confirm their count among each other. Make sure everyone on the crew knows which team was charged with a timeout and how many timeouts each team has left.

Be sure. Two acronyms for you to remember are MIBT and GTBO. Those translate to Make It Be There, and Get the Big One.

There is no place in officiating for guesswork. If you only think you saw a foul, don't throw the flag. In this technological age, virtually every game you work will be videotaped by somebody, be it one of the teams or a parent in the stands. Officials face more scrutiny than ever before. Playoff assignments have been withdrawn over missed calls that showed up on videotape. That's why it's important to avoid phantom calls. If the foul you thought you saw doesn't show up on tape, you could face repercussions. Make It Be There.

Football officials can steal a page from their baseball brethren and use the pause, read and react method of making calls. When you see a potential foul, pause a moment to be sure what you're seeing truly is a foul. Read the act and determine if the foul had a material affect on the play. Ask yourself if game control or fundamental fairness would be compromised if you didn't make the call. After processing that information and answering those questions, you can react by either throwing the flag or making a no-call.

Get The Big One means giving less attention to fouls that don't matter than those that actually affect the game. We're not advocating ignoring the rules. Rather, the idea is to be sure that fouls that give one player or team an advantage over an opponent are penalized. For instance, it's better to adopt a "when in doubt, it's a foul" attitude when dealing with a facemask foul than a uniform number that's the wrong color or style.

Communicate. For some reason, many officials do very little talking on the field, either to players and coaches or to crewmates. They're missing golden opportunities to upgrade their performances.

Wing officials, particularly the line judge, can help the referee by letting him know verbally where a play has ended in relation to the line-to-gain. Simple phrases such as, "They're short," "Take a look; that's pretty close," and "That's a first down," help improve the flow of the game by accelerating the ball-spotting and chain-setting procedures.

Confirm the down with your crewmates after every play. Remind each other of special rules situations such as the fourth-down fumble rule (NCAA) or plays that provide the snapper with protection. If the clock was stopped on the previous play, let the referee know before the ready signal whether the clock starts on the ready or the snap.

Communicate with the coaches when necessary. After a timeout, the wing officials should let the respective coaches know how many timeouts each team has left. Wings should also pass along the numbers of players called for fouls. If the line judge calls a foul on the team whose sideline is on the linesman's side, the linesman should get the number and let the coach know.

Too many officials think the only times captains are necessary are at the coin toss and when it's time to accept or decline a penalty. Make sure you know who the captains are and try to get their names. When talking to them, refer to them as "Mister" or "Captain." Good captains help the officials by taking care of teammates whose actions or comments are bordering on fouls. "Captain Jones, I need some help with your left guard. If I have to, I'll flag him for talking to the opponents, but I'd rather you took care of it so I don't have to."

There are literally dozens of other ways in which communication can make a tough job easier. Don't be afraid to speak up when necessary.

Down and distance. Every official must know the down and distance before every play. That is as basic to football officiating as knowing the count and number of outs in baseball and softball. Understanding how the game strategy is affected by that information (see "Awareness of game situations") is only part of the need to know.

If the chains or down box should be dislodged or moved improperly, or if a complicated penalty enforcement leads to confusion, a crew that knew the down and distance before the play can straighten out the situation without guesswork.

A linesman should never have to turn away from the field to see if a play has ended beyond the line-to-gain. Only by knowing the distance before the play can the linesman know if the line-to-gain was reached. That means no turning around, which in turn leads to good dead-ball officiating.

Here's a play using NFHS rules that demands knowledge of the down. Tie game, 17 seconds on the clock. Team A has the ball, third and 10 on team B's 27 yardline. Team A decides to go for a field goal. The kick is blocked behind the line. The ball never crosses the line of scrimmage and is recovered by the kicking team. Because the kick came on third down, the clock should continue to run. Team A would need to call a timeout in order to get another chance at the field goal. If you mistakenly thought the ball was snapped on fourth down, you would likely stop the clock, giving team A an unfair advantage.

Equipment. The tools of the officiating trade include more than just your uniform and the your flags, beanbags and whistle. Games go more smoothly when officials give thought to other game-related equipment.

For instance, the chains and down box should be checked for each game to be sure they're in good shape. A piece of tape wrapped around the links at the mid-point of the chain helps the linesman when a five-yard foul may or may not give team A a first down. For instance, the first play of a series is a running play that gains five and a half yards. On second down, a team B player crosses the neutral zone and contacts a team A player before the snap. The linesman can look at the chain, see that the down box is slightly beyond the tape and tell the referee that the penalty will result in a first down. That prevents a measurement while still ensuring that team A gets the first down it earned.

The linesman must instruct the chain crew before the game. Some linesmen and many chain crews will give the meeting short shrift because of the experience of the chain gangs or the official. The meeting is important because not every linesman operates in exactly the same way. The meeting should include a reminder to the chain crew regarding safety. If players approach the sideline, the chain crew should be prepared to drop the sticks and move away from the sideline.

At some higher levels of football, the chain crews consist of experienced officials. If you're lucky enough to have such a chain crew in your games, enlist their help. Consider having the person who puts the clip on the chain chart the penalties for your crew. Bring a small clipboard and a chart with spaces listing when the penalty was called, the nature of the foul, which official or officials called it and whether the penalty was accepted or declined. Some conferences or associations require that the report be turned in to a supervisor. Whether or not that is a requirement in your area, the crew can study the information. If you notice that your crew is calling an inordinate number of holding fouls, for instance, a review of the rules regarding blocking may reveal that some of the calls were unnecessary.

Game balls should be inspected before the game to ensure they are properly inflated. When state high school association rules mandate, the ball must have the NFHS authenticating mark. The goalpost pads and pylons should also be checked to be sure they are properly placed.

Consider having the person who puts the clip on the chain chart the penalties for your crew.

This section also refers to player equipment. Before the game, officials should make a casual visual inspection of the players. That can be done while the players are warming up. Issues such as knots in jerseys or tinted eyeshields can be corrected or addressed before the game.

Formation. In addition to down, distance and other game factors, offensive and defensive formations provide hints as to what type of play an official can expect in a given situation. Most teams using the wishbone formation, for instance, are predominantly running teams. Teams using four-receiver sets and shotgun formations pass more times than not.

Defensive formations are less revealing but still helpful. Although teams generally use one defensive alignment such as a 4-3 (four down linemen and three linebackers) or 3-4 (three down linemen and four linebackers) as their base defense, the manner in which they deploy players will depend on what scouting or past experience has determined the opposing offense is likely to do in certain situations.

However, observing the safeties and cornerbacks can provide keys. When a defensive back approaches the line of scrimmage as the quarterback is calling signals, he is "showing blitz." Although teams sometimes fake a blitz, officials can use that key to prepare their coverage for the play. Expect a back to eschew going out for a pass in favor of staying behind the line to help protect the passer. Those blocks can sometimes be double-teams (raising the possibility of a chop block), a cut block (which may be illegal depending on the location of the ball or the players involved when the block occurs) or holds (because not all backs are skilled blockers).

Goalline. When the ball is being snapped from or inside the 10 yardline, be sure you've communicated the information to any official who may have a call involving the goalline. That applies whether the line in question is team A's goalline or team B's goalline.

Referee has long recommended having the wing officials "pinch" the ends. That means moving them closer than normal to the widest player in goalline situations. The mechanic should be used only when the ball is snapped at or inside team B's eight yardline and when the wings are quick and alert enough to avoid being trapped inside if team A runs wide or throws a screen or a pass in the flat. It is also crucial that the wings allow no team A player to line up behind them; the wing should always be outside the widest offensive player.

When the snap is at or inside team B's five yardline, the wings move immediately to the goalline and work back toward the ball if the runner is downed short of the goalline. Don't be afraid to go out of bounds; there is usually more room to work when you get away from the team boxes. Don't hesitate to politely tell photographers, ballboys and other non-team personnel to back up to give you the room you need.

The umpire's role on goalline situations is a subject of great debate. Here's our take on it: Because the umpire is parallel rather than perpendicular to the play, the umpire's position makes it next to impossible to determine the spot or rule whether a touchdown has been scored. (For the same reason, *Referee* believes the umpire should never get forward progress spots elsewhere on the field.) The umpire should get the spot from the covering wing official. That means the umpire will almost never signal a touchdown. Abiding by that mantra means you won't get different signals from the umpire and the wing officials.

The touchdown signal is given only by an official who actually sees the ball in possession of a runner break the plane of the goalline. Mirroring the signal is dangerous; if the covering official is incorrect, the crew will find it difficult to overcome two officials making a mistake. If the covering official is correct, there is no need for a second signal.

The referee must be especially aware of attempts by team A to gain an advantage. Such acts as a rolling start (in which the quarterback walks up behind the snapper and, without stopping, puts his hands under center and immediately receives the snap) and helping the runner must be penalized.

History. Most officials see teams more than once a season or perhaps once every year. The more times you see a team, the more information you can gather and use. Whether it's the type of offense a team runs (such as the wishbone, wing-T, etc.) or a trick play such as a reverse on a kickoff, a little foreknowledge goes a long way. Every game is a history lesson for the gridiron.

Teams have tendencies — strategies, formations and plays they employ in certain situations. For instance, some teams are "right-handed;" they run behind the right tackle on running plays or short-yardage downs. While it would be risky to focus all of your attention on the tackle on such a play, casting your initial glance in that direction gives you an advantage in officiating the play. In the days leading up to a game involving a team that passes the vast majority of the time, a back judge in particular and all officials in general should review the mechanics and rules revolving around pass plays.

History also refers to previous games between the two teams. Perhaps there was an altercation between opponents the last time the teams played. One team may have revenge on its mind after it was blown out or knocked out of the playoffs the previous year. You must still officiate the game with a "clean slate" attitude, but such information should help you recognize potential problems before they arise.

That sort of information should be exchanged during local association meetings. "Our crew has the Tech-Central game this week. Has anyone had either of the teams this year?" "If anyone has the East-West game this week, I can tell you why the papers are full of 'revenge' stories. We had that game last year." Don't embellish the stories or offer an alibi as to why your crew may not have handled a situation as well as you'd have liked. But remember that those who ignore history are doomed to repeat it.

Ineligible and eligible receivers. There are few absolutes in football or in life, but here's one: If a team A player whose number is 50 through 79 inclusive catches a legal forward pass before it's touched by an opponent, you should have a flag on the

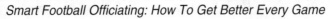

ground. The enforcement will vary depending on which code you're working, where the foul takes place, etc., but it's definitely a foul.

If only everything else involving eligible and ineligible receivers was that easy. The point here is that there are 17 potential eligible receivers on every play that begins with a snap (11 on team B, six on team A). Knowing which players fit which category is crucial. On most plays, that's easy (as noted above). Complications arise when team A uses an unusual formation or the pass is tipped.

There are 17 potential eligible receivers on every play that begins with a snap.

Say you're a wing official and you see team A line up with a wide receiver positioned on the line and a tight end also on the line. That means the tight end is "covered," and is an ineligible pass receiver). That should raise a red flag in your mind — a red flag that should be followed by your gold flag if the tight end is beyond the line of the scrimmage when a legal forward pass crosses the line of scrimmage.

On scoring kick plays in a five-man crew, the back judge and line judge should let each other know the numbers of the eligible receivers on the ends of the line. That way, if a bad snap or a fake results in players moving downfield, the deep officials know who's an eligible receiver.

The umpire should take special note of players taking advantage of the numbering exception on scrimmage kick plays. It's OK for number 18 to snap the ball, but he's an ineligible receiver nonetheless.

Here's one that happens at least once a season, usually in high school freshman games: A player wearing an ineligible number approaches the referee and says, "I'm eligible." You should respond, of course, by clicking on your mike and announcing that tidbit to the world. At least, that's how the NFL guys do it. Unfortunately, only NFL rules allow an ineligible to report as an eligible and high school referees don't (usually) have microphones.

How you respond before the ball is snapped depends on your philosophy. One school of thought says have the referee tell the appropriate wing official, who should try to offer the coach a quick explanation of the rule. Another theory is to let the chips fall where they may; the coach should know the rule. Pick your poison, but remember the rules regarding eligibility.

Jog. A phrase to remember: Don't walk when you can jog and don't jog when you should run.

Wing officials who come into the middle of the field to provide a spot or report a penalty should jog back to the sideline. Officials should jog to their positions for a free kick or after a timeout. Don't sprint in those situations, which is often construed as false hustle. Save sprinting for covering a play.

Wing officials who are not responsible for the forward progress spot (such as on a sweep to the other side) have to observe the players not directly involved in the play. That's called "cleaning up after the play." As the players move downfield, move down with them, not ahead of them. That usually requires only a jog as well.

Keys. Another fundamental of officiating is knowing and observing your keys. By observing keys, officials can discern the type of play, which ensures that players involved in the play will be observed.

Keys are predetermined by the position you are working in the game and can be discerned when team A lines up in its formation. For instance, in a five-man crew, the back judge's

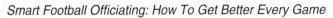

main key is the widest eligible receiver outside the tackle on the strong side of the formation (that will usually be a split end). At the snap, the back judge observes the actions of his key player. If that player moves into another official's coverage area, the back judge gives him up and shifts his attention to players who have entered his coverage area.

In order to determine keys, the officials must recognize the strength of the formation (strong side vs. weak side). Strength has nothing to do with the number (or size) of the offensive linemen on each side of the center. The strong side is the side on which there are more eligible receivers outside of the tackle. The vast majority of the time, that will be the side on which the tight end lines up.

In regard to determining keys, it doesn't matter if a player is on or off the line of scrimmage. For instance, the player closest to the tackle is the back judge's key whether the player is a tight end (directly next to the tackle) or a wide out (split outside the tackle). If players are stacked, the player nearest the line of scrimmage is considered to be the widest. For example, if a wingback is stacked directly behind the tight end, the tight end is considered the widest and is the wing official's key.

The back judge has priority in determining keys, followed by the wing men. Wing officials should not key the same player as the back judge.

The umpire and referee rely on linemen for their keys. Pulling linemen indicate a sweep or a trap block. Retreating linemen indicate a pass. Charging linemen indicate a running play. When offensive linemen provide only passive resistance, allowing defensive linemen to penetrate the neutral zone, a screen pass often follows.

The referee observes the running backs and quarterback prior to the snap. Once the ball is snapped, he looks through the quarterback to the opposite side tackle. For instance, if the quarterback is right-handed and the referee is properly stationed to the quarterback's right, the key is the left tackle.

The umpire observes the snapper and the guards prior to the snap, then shifts his look to the opposite tackle after the snap. If the keys indicate a run, the umpire must determine the point of attack. A double team or a trap block often occur at the point of attack. Likewise, pulling guards often provide the interference for a sweep or reverse.

Use your keys and you'll go a long way to proper coverage of every play.

Lighten up. Officiating is a serious business, but that doesn't mean it can't have lighter moments. When you meet the captains, greet them with a smile and a handshake. Use your body language to give the impression that you're approachable.

If a coach or a player cracks a joke during a dead-ball period, respond with a smile or a chuckle. We're not advocating that you respond with a belly laugh or a stand-up comedy routine. But don't feel that you have to be the great stoneface every minute you're on the field.

There are times when levity is not appropriate. Those situations include but are not limited to injury timeouts (you don't want anyone to think you're making light of an injury), a discussion with a coach (smiling during an argument sends the message that you're not taking the coach's comments seriously) and a blowout game (don't make it appear as if you're making fun of the losing team).

If the halftime or postgame conversation among the officials involves a call that may have been missed, don't be afraid to admit a mistake. Accepting responsibility for errors is one step on the road to learning and ensuring that the mistake isn't repeated.

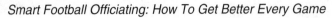

Stand your ground if you think you're right. But if evidence suggests that you were wrong, don't be so stubborn or prideful that you compound the error.

Motion. When a team A player goes in motion, every official on the field should take notice. Before the snap, the official away from whom the player is moving has to make sure the man in motion doesn't cut upfield before the snap. The referee has to make sure team A doesn't have to men in motion. The back judge has to know if the motion has change the strength of the formation because that will change his key (see "Keys"). Officials should also notice how team B responds to the motion. Perhaps defensive backs that had been close to the line of scrimmage and ready to blitz will drop off.

Once the ball is snapped, the player in motion still bears attention. Motion men are often used as lead blockers on sweeps. Make sure someone watches that block to make sure it's legal. See the entire block so you don't penalize team A for contact that starts above the waist and ends below the waist or starts in the front and ends in the back only because the team B player turned.

Notes. "Cheat sheets" were discouraged during your school days, but they come in handy on the football field. Most officials pull out their information card before the game, jot down the captains' numbers, record which team won the toss and put the card back into their pocket. They don't look at it again until the second half unless a team takes a timeout before halftime. That's an incredible waste of a potentially valuable resource.

Record the captains' names (first and last) and numbers. Players will be more responsive when called by their name rather than number. If you need a captain's help in dealing with an exuberant teammate, the captain will be more receptive if called by his name. If the coach doesn't offer the captains' names in the pregame meeting, ask for them.

Jot down the results of the coin toss. You might also consider recording which captain served as his team's spokesman. If the coach wanted his captain to defer the choice but the player chose to receive, the coach will want to speak to the captain who disobeyed his orders. Write down both team's choices. If you're confused about which compass direction the teams are facing, use S for scoreboard end and N for non-scoreboard end, if applicable.

Log the number of the player who asked for a timeout and the time on the clock when the timeout was granted.

Record the name or number of any ejected player or coach. In games using NFHS rules, record the name or number of any player who was knocked unconscious. If a doctor signs a statement allowing the player to return, note the time the player returned to the game.

Every official should note the down, distance and position of the ball (i.e. left hash, slightly right of center) at the end of the first and third quarters. That information will help you reset the ball properly to start the next quarter.

The card also provides a means of jotting down reminders for discussion at halftime or after the game. If you are unsure you properly applied a rule, when time allows make a note to yourself to check on it. If you think of a way your crew can better cover a certain type of play, you can write it down.

Umpires may wish to record the uniform numbers of players they inspected before the game. It will help an umpire remember which players had equipment that was judged illegal should the player participate wearing the illegal gear.

If you find all of this information won't fit on a standard information card, create your own or use a blank index card. Another tip: When working a game in rain or snow, take along a plastic bag with a reusable seal such as a sandwich bag. Keeping the card in the sealed bag will limit the amount of time it is exposed to the elements.

Out of bounds. One of the toughest things to teach newer officials is the need to turn away from the field of play when a play ends out of bounds. Some less-experienced officials seem to think that no one will see them give the stop-the-clock signal unless they are facing the field. Others worry about what's going on behind them, not realizing that other officials are (or should be) observing players still on the field.

You may see 99 plays ending out of bounds with no problems. But that 100th play could be the one in which someone delivers a blow after the whistle. If you don't see it and the act goes unpenalized, you may soon find yourself breaking up a brawl.

At no time while players are out of bounds should officials turn their backs on the play. Never allow players who have crossed the sideline return to the field without an official accompanying them. Holding the spot with your foot, blowing your whistle, signaling the clock to stop and watching the players may seem like a lot do at one time, but it comes naturally with practice.

Wing officials often feel they are restricted and must stay on the field during play. That is not the case. If for no other reason than safety, wings should not hesitate to move beyond the sideline when necessary, such as when a sweep or sideline pass brings several players toward the sideline. That's why it's important for wing officials to keep a "clean sideline," one in which players and coaches stand only where allowed by rule.

Linesmen and line judges can improve their chances of clean sidelines by having each head coach designate a "get-back coach." The get-back coach is usually an assistant coach who urges substitutes, trainers and other sideline personnel to stay in the team boxes.

The wing official should introduce himself to the get-back coach shortly before the game begins. If, in the excitement of the game, the get-back coach forgets his duties, a gentle reminder from the wing official usually does the trick. Players will usually respond to a coach's order to get back.

Postgame. Another longtime *Referee* emphasis has been the importance of a pregame meeting. Less discussed but equally important is the postgame meeting.

Once the game is over and you've reached the locker room, a crew should honestly assess its performance. If an unusual play occurred, discuss how it was handled and if the reaction was correct. Even if it was a routine game, the crew can discuss what it did well and what it could have done better.

Be technical and be critical. Don't let the conversation deteriorate into a testosterone festival, filled with comments like, "Did you hear what I told that coach? Man, I shut him up in a hurry!" Instead, examine what caused the blowup. "The coach said I missed a clip on that kickoff return for a touchdown. Did any of you see it? I saw the block and thought it was legal. Should I have told the coach I saw it and passed on it?"

Be technical and be critical.

One of the more pleasant aspects of officiating is going out for food and beverages after a game. You can discuss elements of the game over dinner, but be careful. Other restaurant patrons may have attended the game. You don't want to start a debate with fans or air your dirty laundry in a potentially hostile area. What's said in the locker room should stay there.

Quiet word. Just as a picture says a thousand words, a look or brief comment can work wonders on the football field. The quiet word is part of preventive officiating. If you see an offensive lineman hold an opponent on a play on which the run goes to the other side of the field, let the lineman know you saw it. "Hey, number 76. Understand that if you hold like that at the point of attack, I'll have to throw a flag." If a player is acting up but has not yet earned a flag, talk to him. "Come on now, 55. You're a better player than that. Play football, OK?" Use a conversational tone, not an aggressive tone.

You say that sounds like you're coaching? Au contraire. You're passing along information. Officials are not merely enforcers; part of their job is to improve or at least maintain the flow of the game.

The quiet word doesn't have to be punitive. If a runner hands you the ball instead of making you bend for it, say thank you. If a player helps an opponent to his feet, compliment him for that act of good sportsmanship.

There will be times when you'll need to raise your voice in order to make a point. But that should happen as little as possible. There will also be times when you should not speak at all. Sometimes merely making eye contact with a player or coach is all that is necessary to convey the message you choose to send.

Rulebook. Believe it or not, the rulebook is more of a friend than an enemy. The vast majority of the questions you have about situations can be answered simply by checking in the rulebook. The trick is knowing where to look. It comes easily only by reading and re-reading the book.

When you get your new rulebook, speed-read the entire book. Read it as if you're cruising through a novel. You will not remember everything you read, but don't worry about that now. Familiarize yourself with different sections so you don't need to rely on the index.

Categorize the rules. Some rules have more game-to-game impact than others. For example, the "Game, Field Players and

Equipment" rules, often near the front of the book, are not necessarily the ones you should read first. While important, that section is not the most important for someone who is trying to learn the rules. What's more important, a legal blocking technique or the width of the stripes on the ball? Perhaps the most important section of the book is the one dedicated to definitions. Mastering the definitions not only helps you on the field, it helps you study the rest of the book.

Read in short increments of time. After the initial reading of the entire rulebook, study in increments of 15-20 minutes per sitting. Digest the material in bite-sized pieces. Read some part of the rulebook each day, including during the offseason. Make it as much a part of your daily routine as brushing your teeth.

Study just before falling asleep. Studies have shown that memory retention is enhanced by studying right before sleeping. Instead of watching TV as you begin to fall asleep, read the rulebook.

Don't forget to check related casebook plays or approved rulings. Once you've grasped a rule, read related caseplays and manuals before moving to the next rule. Caseplays enhance knowledge by taking rules and placing them into game situations. However, the caseplays cannot replace the rulebook. Also, take quizzes and tests, which reinforce what you already know or emphasize what you don't know.

Keep your rulebook near your TV. If a foul occurs, ask yourself how the penalty would be enforced at the level you work. Check the rulebook to make sure you're correct.

Signals. Clear, sharp signals not only help public address announcers, teams and spectators understand what call has been made, they enhance the impression an official makes in the eyes of others.

The hand signals used by football referees to signify penalties can be traced to the late 1920s. In a game between Syracuse and Cornell, radio announcer Ted Husing asked referee Ellwood Geiges if Geiges could do something to keep the press booth informed of the action. Some of the signals Geiges created on the spot (such as offside and holding) are still used in their original form. Albie Booth, a well-known official of that era, is also credited with originating many of the signals.

Ideally, you want to appear poised and relaxed when giving signals. You do not want to create the impression you are lethargic or lazy. The other extreme, appearing overly excited, should also be avoided. Avoid nervous mannerisms such as tugging on your lanyard, repeatedly snapping your down indicator, etc. Have the same body language late in the game as you had at the beginning and, above all, avoid getting caught up in the emotion of the game.

Neither your signals nor your facial expression should indicate emotion. If you've just flagged a coach for unsportsmanlike conduct or ejected a player, over-enthusiastic thrusts of the arms can enflame an already contentious situation.

Avoid nervous mannerisms such as tugging on your lanyard.

Add some emphasis to your signals when you're trying to sell a close call. But save that emphasis for occasions when it is needed. In all other instances, maintain a slow, even tempo.

Some associations allow supplemental signals. Check with your association before using such non-authorized signals.

Your signals must be firm, but not flashy. Don't give signals that infer a "gotcha" attitude to the offending player.

Timers. Few things make an official's life more miserable than a bad clock operator. If the clock stops or starts incorrectly despite the officials' best efforts and signals, the officials will bear the brunt of coaches' wrath, not the timer.

In extreme cases, officials can take over the timing of a game. But that should be an absolute last resort, one undertaken only if the timer is clearly trying to influence the outcome of the game (which is difficult if not impossible to prove).

Confirm the starting time.

Before going to the pressbox to meet the timer in the pregame, the appropriate official must confirm with the game manager the starting time of the game and the length of halftime. That information should also be confirmed with the timer.

It is preferable to have the clock expire before the scheduled starting time. If coordinated properly, the introduction of starting lineups or other pregame ceremonies will be concluded so that the starting time will not be delayed. Example: Game time is 7:30 p.m. and the introductions and national anthem take roughly 10 minutes to complete. The clock should hit zero at 7:20 p.m. That system is preferable but is rarely used at most levels.

On free kicks, remind the timer to wait for the proper signal. From scrimmage, the clock will start either with the referee's ready or on the snap.

Remind the timer that five signals should cause him to stop the clock: stop the clock, incomplete pass, touchdown, touchback and safety.

The timer must observe the covering official on plays that end at the sideline. If the covering official gives the start-the-clock signal to indicate the ball is inbounds and then signals to stop the clock, the timer must understand that the sequence means the clock will next start on the ready. Also remind the timer to look for

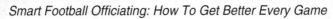

the stop-the-clock signal when the ball goes near a sideline, there is a change of possession or there is a first down, and that trys are always untimed.

Instruct the timer to wait for the referee's signal before starting the countdown for halftime. That signal is contingent upon both teams clearing the field. For NFHS games, there is an additional three-minute warmup that immediately follows the intermission. That time should also start on the referee's signal so he can ensure both teams are on the field ready to loosen up.

Another item for prep games: If the regulation game ends in a tie and overtime is played, the timer will need to put three minutes on the clock (NFHS rules mandate a three-minute break between the end of regulation play and the first overtime period) and again wait for the referee's signal. After that, the clock is not needed unless there is a second overtime (a two-minute break occurs in that case).

The timer should be asked how the referee will be able to communicate with the timer if the clock needs to be corrected. In some cases, assistant coaches in the pressbox communicate through headphones to coaches on the sideline. Using the coaches is one method of relaying information. Another is to have the referee signal the correct time with his fingers, like a basketball official reporting a foul to the scorer. The official meeting with the timer should find out if the clock is programmable (can be set to a specific time) or if it has to a run through a one-minute cycle in order to be reset.

The timer should also be asked if the clock is in working order to the best of his knowledge. If there were mechanical malfunctions in previous weeks, were the problems solved? Either way, *Referee* recommends having an official on the field (usually the back judge in a five-man crew or the line judge in a four-man crew) time the game as a backup. If the clock malfunctions during the game, the timer should be instructed to wait for a timeout or other break in the action before resetting the clock. The timer should communicate with the referee to obtain the correct time, then reset the clock.

In areas using a game-shortening procedure (such as a 35-point rule), it's a good idea to provide the timer with a list of exceptions to clock rules.

Uniform. The editors at *Referee* have harped on wearing the correct uniform and using the proper accessories for so long, it seems redundant to bring it up again here. Yet year after year there are reports of officials wearing dirty, ill-fitting, old or improper uniforms, unpolished shoes, adjustable caps and committing other fashion faux pas. One crew showed up for a state playoff football game wearing V-neck basketball shirts. Another group featured three of the officials wearing uniform socks with stirrups and the other two wearing one-piece socks. That crew also had four members in long-sleeved shirts and one wearing short sleeves.

> **Provide the timer with a list of exceptions to clock rules.**

Apparently the message has not gotten through to everybody, so here goes again.

The standard black and white shirt with a Byron collar and one-inch vertical stripes are worn. Leave the wide-stripe shirts for the guys who've made it to the NFL. Officials should own shirts with short and long sleeves. All crew members should wear the same length sleeves. Do not wear a long-sleeved garment underneath a short-sleeved shirt. T-shirts and turtlenecks (for cold weather) should be black. The undershirt should not have any letters or pictures that could be seen through your striped shirt. Shirts should always be tucked in. Association patches are allowed if it's accepted in the area.

Knickers should be clean, white (not yellowed) with a black belt. The overlap at the bottom of the knickers should not be more than four inches below the knee. The belt must be black, one and one-quarter to two inches wide, with a nondescript buckle. When state associations allow, white shorts may be worn. Knickers are standard attire for college games and scrimmages. White compression shorts should be worn underneath the knickers. Shirts should be tucked inside the compression shorts to prevent stripes from showing through the knickers.

Entirely black shoes are most acceptable; however, some state associations and college conferences allow black with minimal white markings (like shoe logos). Black laces are always worn.

The one-piece football stocking is almost universally worn. The NFHS requires socks with northwestern stripes (one-half inch white, one-half inch black, one inch white, one-half inch black, one-half inch white). The width of the black showing below the knickers should be the same as the wide black band below the striping pattern. The Collegiate Commissioners Association (CCA), which sets the standards for college officials, specifies that the white portion of the sock above the top of the shoe heel should be between three and four inches wide. A black portion above the white should be between two and two and one-quarter inches wide. The alternating black and white stripes should be one-half to five-eighths of an inch wide. The black between the top of the top white stripes and the bottom of the knickers should be between two and two and one-quarter inches wide.

A black cap with white piping should be worn by all but the referee. The referee's white hat must be clean. All caps should be fitted and made of either wool or nylon. Adjustable caps and those made of mesh appear unprofessional.

The CCA does not allow jackets to be worn during games. When high school associations allow jackets to be worn during the game, the jacket should be black and white striped. Jackets may be worn before the game during warmups. All officials should either wear jackets or go without. *Referee* strongly recommends that jackets not be worn during games. There are plenty of undergarments on the market that will keep you warm. An official wearing a jacket just doesn't look as professional as one not wearing one.

Do not go to the game dressed in any part of your uniform. It just looks unprofessional. Make a good first impression on game management by wearing clean, pressed clothes to and from the game. Jeans, shorts, T-shirts, baseball caps, sneakers, shorts, sandals, sweatsuits and jogging attire are inappropriate. Wedding rings may be worn on the field, but other rings, necklaces, bracelets and earrings may not. As a backup in case a watch malfunctions during the game, at least one official who doesn't have timing responsibilities should wear a watch.

Carry your uniform in a garment bag or gym bag. The bag should be neat (no frayed edges, etc.) and entirely black. Some associations have their group's logo or the official's name embroidered on the bag. That's acceptable if that's what officials in the area are doing. If no one else in the area is doing it, don't do it just to stand out.

Many officials at the high school and college levels use all black, wheeled, airline-type luggage. They keep your clothes clean and pressed and, because of the wheels, are easy to transport.

Video. Whenever possible, watch tape of the games you work. Most athletic directors and coaches will gladly send a copy of the game tape if the crew provides a blank tape along with a self-addressed, postage-paid video mailer. The crew should chip in and share the expenses since everyone on the crew will benefit.

Another way to obtain a videotape is to simply have someone use a camcorder to tape your game. An added benefit to that method is that the person doing the shooting can focus more on the officials than on the game action. It is best to get another official to do the taping because an official knows what's best to tape.

Once you get the tape, watch it with a critical eye, preferably as a crew. Questions you should be asking include: Are you lining up where you should be? After the ball is snapped, are you moving to be in position to make the necessary calls? Are you looking off the ball or are you being a ball watcher? How are your forward-progress spots?

Check to make sure penalties were properly enforced, the crew correctly signaled the clock to stop and start, flags and beanbags were dropped at the appropriate places and that the fouls you called actually show up on film.

Whistle. Your whistle is like your voice. It can convey messages, in a "whisper" or a "holler." When you blow your whistle, make sure you're saying what you want to say. The ready-for-play signal should be a firm, one- or two-second tone. A request for a timeout or some other clock stoppage merits a firmer if not longer blast. When an official has thrown or sees a penalty flag on a play, a series of short toots help inform the referee of the situation.

Now about the whistle itself. If a whistle on a lanyard is used, both must be black. Carry a spare in your pants pocket. If a finger whistle is used, it should also be black plastic. Use a finger whistle only if you've trained yourself not to make one-armed signals.

Finger whistles are a boon for several reasons. One is safety. With the whistle out of your mouth, you are less likely to have teeth knocked out or damaged if a player's stray elbow hits you in the mouth. Another reason is preventing inadvertent whistles. The time it takes you to bring your whistle to your mouth is all the time it may take to realize you shouldn't be blowing the whistle at all.

Xerophilous. You probably wondered how we were going to solve the "X" problem. Now you're probably wondering what the heck xerophilous is and how it relates to officiating.

Our friends at Webster's tell us that xerophilous means "Capable of thriving in a hot, dry climate." Some plants and animals are so equipped, but most humans are not. To make a long story short, this is a reminder to drink plenty of fluids when you officiate in hot or humid weather.

Dehydration is arguably the most dangerous side effect of officiating in hot conditions for prolonged periods of time. Dehydration can not only dramatically affect performance, but can lead to heat stroke, a potentially life-threatening condition.

When exercise is performed in high humidity, sweat doesn't evaporate as efficiently to produce cooling. The increase in body temperature causes more ineffective sweating, increases dehydration and hastens the increase in core body temperature. The combination of increased body temperature and rapid dehydration leads to decreased performance.

A drop in physical ability is not the only consequence of even slight dehydration. Several scientific studies have shown dehydration also leads to decreased mental ability.

Sports officials are faced with complex tasks requiring judgment, memory and concentration. Considering the loss of mental ability and physical performance, a dehydrated official will not only be unable to run to the action, he won't know what to do when he gets there.

Avoiding dehydration is difficult because athletes and officials will typically take a drink only when thirsty. Quenching your thirst does not sufficiently replenish fluid levels. Avoiding dehydration requires drinking more fluid than needed to satisfy thirst.

Drinks containing sugar and salt are an official's best fluid replacement. A number of these "sports drinks" are available and all contain reasonable amounts of both carbohydrates (sugars) and electrolytes (salts). Avoid soda-type drinks since most contain too much sugar and not enough salts. Sodas also contain caffeine, which increases urine production and counteracts your body's effort to conserve water.

Ideally, you should consume four to six ounces of fluid for every 10 to 15 minutes of activity to effectively avoid dehydration. That avoids filling the stomach with large quantities of fluid at one time. Most officials cannot stop activity every few minutes to take a drink. A more practical technique is to drink three to four cups (24 to 32 ounces) of fluid about once an hour. Use that method in your preseason workouts in order to get your body accustomed to performing activities with fluid in your stomach.

According to Dr. Emilio Vazquez, M.D., who practices family medicine and officiates in Madisonville, Ky., drinking about two or three cups of fluid 10 to 15 minutes before a game is also recommended. Over-hydration will not only decrease the chance of dehydration, but will also help your stomach start emptying and force your body to absorb the fluid. If it's a very hot or humid day, increase fluid intake to as much as one to two quarts an hour.

Replenishing lost fluids after a contest is important when an official has an assignment the following day. Even under ideal circumstances, it's difficult to end a long day sufficiently hydrated. If you start the next day a little "dried out," you'll have a hard time catching up with your body's needs.

Yesterday. As the old saying goes, you're only as good as your last game. Many officials work more than one game each week. The last game you worked — yesterday's game, if you will — is gone. If you experienced problems in that previous game, you can't carry the problems over to your next game. The same with your last call. If you kick one, forget about it for the moment. If you let it eat at you, you won't be thinking about the next call and you'll kick that one, too.

The time to dwell on your mistakes and examine your performance is after the game. Solicit advice from crewmates, mentors or veteran officials whose opinions you trust. Fix the problem, then get on with your life.

Zebra. There may still be places were "zebra" is still used as a derogatory term to describe officials. But in most areas officials use it to describe themselves. It's a badge of honor. Some officials have personal stationary emblazoned with zebras. They've chosen to turn a negative image into a positive one.

Officials should take pride in their avocation. That means being a professional at all times, not just when you're in uniform. Unacceptable behavior brings disrepute to the entire officiating community. Officials should be role models.

2

Sound Advice
from Solid Refs

By Jeffrey Stern

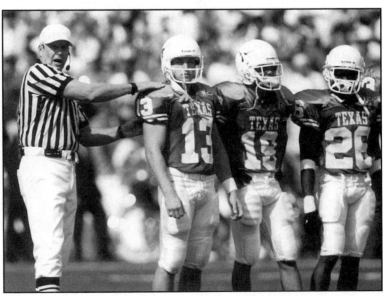

Randy Christal, Texas

In the more than 25 years that *Referee* has been published, readers have been treated to interviews and feature stories involving dozens of top officials. Those articles have included many tips and pieces of advice that are not only timeless but helpful to any official at any level.

In this chapter, some prominent officials share their thoughts on what it takes to be a successful official. As you'll see, it takes more than a clean uniform and mere experience.

NFL referee Gerald Austin, a veteran of three Super Bowls, discusses supporting your crew and being a leader:

"I think the first responsibility (of a referee) is to support your crew members. If you're going to function as a unit, they've got to believe that they can trust their leader. We all want to be able to trust our leader.

"I do a lot of leadership training. One of the first things I say is, 'A leader is no more than a facilitator, and facilitators can only go as far as the followers are willing to go.' If the followers say, 'I'm not going there,' no matter what, the leader says you're not going. They've got to believe and have confidence in the leader, and part of that confidence is the leader showing reverse support for the followers. You've got to have that support for your crew.

"A leader is no more than a facilitator."

"When you're representing a crew member to the league office, because that's the lines of communication, you've got to be supportive of that person. If it's borderline, then I'm going to support the crew member. If it's obvious that the crew member made a mistake, then I'm going to support what's right and talk to the crew member and say, 'I can't carry this; I don't feel comfortable carrying this to the league office because I don't feel you're correct.' We'll talk about it within the crew. ...We try to get the entire crew to say whether they agree with the grade or they disagree."

Bill Carollo

Bill Carollo, an NFL official since 1989, recalls how he learned from a mistake in a game early in his NCAA Division I career:

"There was 1:26 left in the game. I thought, 'This is easy.' I'm 28 years old, there are 60,000 people in the stands. I had an offensive pass interference, I was the only guy who got 12 on the field on defense. I had a holding call, and I thought, 'I can do this.' I was really confident.

"And the very next play, Wisconsin punted and about 12 people muffed the ball and before I knew it the ball was in the end zone, and I'm whistling touchback because it broke the plane. And then I realized in the college rule, it isn't dead immediately. And I killed it because I was still just learning high schools rules and I was just getting into college.

"So (the crew) had a big conference, got it straightened out, and it was a huge embarrassment. But it was a great lesson for me that if you move too fast, you can shorten your career very quickly. I got a lot of attention. I admitted that I made a mistake but we corrected it. We gave them a touchdown on the play.

"I learned a lot from that one play. For one, I didn't know the rules. I'm out in the game and I wasn't prepared. So probably the biggest thing I learned is, even though you're young, you can study the rules all week long. Maybe the game is only on Saturday or Sunday for three hours, but you've got the whole week to prepare. And I don't think there's a good excuse. We're all human and we make mistakes, but you shouldn't make too many mistakes on rules. That's just a matter of studying and memorizing and trying to apply the right rule in the right situation.

"I think if you learn and you bounce back, it isn't so much that you made the mistake. They don't want you to make the same mistake a second time. And, more importantly, they want to see how you react the next time you walk out on that field, if you're going to be totally gun-shy. Are you afraid to throw a flag because you threw it last time and you were wrong? Or the coach yelled at you and you're afraid to throw the flag next time because he's screaming at you?"

Veteran Big 12 referee Randy Christal, whose bowl assignments include the 1992 national championship game, on dealing with coaches:

"Never go to one coach unless you go to the other coach because they have these complexes. Let them know what's going on. Get your crew to talk to them. I don't mean a running conversation, but if they've asked something, be respectful and give them a response. Be darn sure we get them numbers (of players who are called for fouls). I tell them in the pregame, 'When the umpire and I go in and talk to them, if there's something unusual, I will come over and explain it to you. And if you see me explaining to one coach, hang on, I'm going to be coming to you to explain it.' Just let them know. And I'll say, 'You may not know what we've called, but I want you to know the who, what, when, where and why that we called it.' Then, I always say, 'If you'll just keep your assistants back, this is between you and me.' They're all very receptive to that. They like the feeling that they can talk to you."

Tony Corrente

NFL referee Tony Corrente recalls an incident in a college game that provided lessons on recognizing trouble before it starts:

"I was the referee at a Utah State-BYU game. BYU had a big lead. Ty Detmer was the BYU quarterback. He got hit on a play and he and a linebacker were face-to-face on the ground and they were exchanging words. (Detmer) got up and everything was fine. The very next play, the same linebacker blitzes in the same manner and puts (Detmer) on his back and they start scuffling. And before I can get the two of them separated, both of them are in the middle of the field at Utah State with a major brawl taking place. We ejected a few players and settled things right down.

"The feeling in the pit of my stomach was, 'You gotta be kidding me. Why is everybody coming out here?' Because it really didn't start out as anything major. You had a young man with a score that was out of hand at that point and (BYU was) still throwing the ball. So you had animosity with an interstate rivalry and all that that takes place. One team had had enough and the other team was angry.

"I learned a great deal about just being aware of the potential for the kinds of eruptions that can take place. It really is game flow. It teaches you to not just be aware of time and place, down and distance, but all the things associated with the game. It's maintaining the flow of the game and being aware of the circumstances. It's really attempting to be aware and attuned so you can prevent those catastrophic things from happening."

Former California Highway Patrolman (CHP) Al Jury is a retired NFL field judge. He has worked five Super Bowls. Here's his take on the importance of dead-ball officiating:

"Years ago, the Minnesota Vikings were playing San Diego. (Minnesota receiver) Ahmad Rashad was the wideout on my side. They had a defensive back who was back off of him about 12 yards. (Quarterback Tommy) Kramer comes up and takes the snap, and throws the ball to the opposite side of the field. I looked at the pass and while I was looking, this guy closes in and I never see it. By the time I turn around, Rashad is laying on his back.

"Now Carl Eller and Alan Page and those guys (on the Viking sideline) are yelling at me, 'Didn't you see that?' Trainers are on the field. I walk up and Rashad has got a grin on his face, so I'm thinking to myself, 'It couldn't have been that bad.'

"The next week we get the critique sheet, and (then-supervisor of officials) Art McNally writes on the sheet, 'How could you miss this?'

"Art McNally writes on the sheet, 'How could you miss this?'"

"What happened was, when I looked away, this guy just closed and took a shot to Rashad. If I had seen it, I would've thrown him out of the game. He caught him with a forearm to the head and knocked him down.

"Now I tell guys, 'Keep your head on a swivel.' I learned from that, and it's never happened to me again. Although nothing's happening to that receiver, he's still your primary responsibility, so if you look up, you'd better look back right away.

"It cost me dearly, because I probably didn't get a playoff game that year because of that. It was bad enough that Art made a comment on that. It didn't hurt me, because two years later I was in the Super Bowl. But the point I'm making is, fish in your own pond. Look for your own responsibility. Your primary responsibility is nobody's but yours. If you look away to help somewhere else, don't forget about this guy. I put my head on a swivel now. Even though I might look away, I'm going to hurry up and look back to see what's going on with my guy."

John Laurie's long NCAA Division I career included numerous bowl games. He is well known for an extensive pregame conference that includes visual elements. He describes the process:

"I developed a little flip card set on a spiral notebook and I flip them over. There are 71 things and I say 95 percent of what happens in this football game today will be a part of 71 of these things that we're going to cover, and the other five percent, somebody has got to step up and make sure we get it right.

"Never end with confusion."

"The first play I might say was an eight-yard gain off-tackle. What's our positioning? The second play was 15 yards. How far down the field is the line judge going to go to cover that play?

"I would tell all officials, particularly those just getting started, it's so damn easy for someone to talk about the duck that flies over that a punt hits or whatever. But just avoid that. Here I am in 22 years of major college football and I'm trying to find the 71 things that are going to happen the most often in a football game and make sure every one of those we get right. If we have great mechanics and we have good movement among the officials in terms of covering positions, we know exactly who is shutting the clock down, we know exactly where we're going on penalty enforcement, we know exactly what we're going to do on disqualification, the things that can happen in a football game, you're so much farther ahead.

"A part of my pregame is to never end with confusion. If we have an issue come up in a pregame that no one is sure of or whatever, I'll just assign an official to stop, read the book and catch up with us and give us an interpretation later. You want them to end with more confidence than when they started. And to do that you have to make them feel comfortable and show at the end that there's an opportunity for everybody to come together on agreement on the things that are going to happen in the game."

REFEREE

Bill LeMonnier

Veteran Big 10 referee Bill LeMonnier talks about the onfield and off-field pressures in major college officiating:

"I was working in the Gateway Conference and was an alternate on the Big 10 staff. (Big 10 supervisor of officials) David Parry called and asked what was the biggest crowd I had worked in front of in the Gateway. I said, 'Maybe about 17,000 at Northern Iowa.' And he said, 'Well, I'm going to send you out to Penn State and there's going to be about 94,000 out there. Do you think you can handle it?' I told him I'd bring an extra pair of pants; in case there was a problem I'd be able to change them.

"He came back with a pretty solid piece of advice for me. He said, 'I want you to remember something: 94,000 people are going to scream loud and they're going to scream long. And if they're really upset with you, they'll even scream for two or three plays. But that crowd won't hire you and that crowd won't fire you.'

"He said, 'You're going to feel a lot worse when you go to a Wednesday night film review and I show them a film. I'll say that our new back judge, Bill LeMonnier, makes this pass interference call that's not pass interference. You're going to feel a lot worse in front of 40 of your peers than you're going to ever feel in front of 94,000 people. The sooner you get the crowd out of your head, the sooner you're going to have a good game out there.'

"He was absolutely right. It's a football game and it's blocking and tackling and passing and running just like any other level, just faster."

Retired NFL referee Bob McElwee on the importance of study:

"(Officiating is) easier to do the better prepared you are. If you know what you're doing, there's no question that (players and coaches) are going to find out that you know what you're doing, and things are going to be a little bit different when they do. You can do what you want between Monday and Saturday, but I'm telling you right now in the long run, they're going to find out.

"We have a hundred and some great officials, but (the teams) are going to find out who the best ones are, and they're going to find out who knows and who doesn't know. If you want to take that risk, you're crazy, but I'm not taking that risk. It requires a lot of sacrifice. I was an avid reader, and I still love to read, but I don't read anything near what I used to read before I got in the NFL because I read our stuff. I read our rulebook, I read our mechanics book. You have to be constantly drumming that stuff into your head, because when it happens, it's going to happen so fast, if it's not automatic you're not going to get it."

Dave Parry, Big 10 supervisor and national supervisor of college officiating, talks about the perils of over-officiating:

"College officials have a tendency to get themselves in more hot water when they over-officiate than when they under-officiate. I talk to commissioners and other supervisors. We all share our problems. It seems that people really get burned when somebody has a foul or an interpretation that's way too technical or way too literal. They've got a head linesman throwing pass interference on the other side of the field 60 yards away from him. Three officials looked at it and said, 'That's not a foul,' and this guy from way downtown throws the flag. And now the coach is really outraged.

"Well, why would this guy call it when these other three guys don't? And then you look at the play and inevitably it's very, very marginal. One of our biggest concerns is to train and educate the men to not be overly technical, not be overly literal, to have a great feel for the game, common-sense football approach.

"There are just times in a football game when football sense has to take over rather than literal sense. Officiating is part science and part art. I think the art part is the most important. Get just the big ones and make them be there.

"Officiating is part science and part art."

The game is for the kids and the coaches and the fans. We're not out there to draw attention to ourselves. If we get that message across, I think we'd be better off."

Retired NFL referee Jim Tunney describes how working with Special Olympians inspired him to work harder to be a better referee:

"I saw an 11-year-old girl. Her name was Evelyn. She won the three-meter diving championship. She was blind. Next time you've got a tough decision to make, the next time you get that fear in your belly, you wonder if you have the guts, the courage, to make that decision, stop and think about Evelyn climbing up a ladder she can't see, walking out to the end of a board and diving into a pool of water that somebody told her was there.

"I saw an athlete with cerebral palsy so bad that he had no use of either hand and one leg. He was sitting in a wheelchair, and he could only reach the ground with his left foot, so he turned his wheelchair around and pushed it backwards and raced 25 meters. It took him eight minutes, and he finished third. He was ecstatic that he'd finished third. He was 59 years of age. Too late to keep on keeping on? You've been around a long time, you've been the same for 25 years or more, so many of you. Is it too late to take it to the next level?

"I saw a 26-year-old mentally, physically and emotionally challenged young man standing on the victory stand because he had just won his age category in the 100-meter dash. The judge put a ribbon around his neck. With the gold medal hanging there, this young man said, 'Thanks.' I was standing not far away. I turned to the sponsor, tears coming down her cheeks. I said, 'You know, that's a marvelous accomplishment for that young man.' She said, 'Yes, it's a great accomplishment, but that's the first word he's ever spoken.'"

Red Cashion

Retired NFL referee Red Cashion talks about the positive aspects as well as the regrets of a long, successful career:

"I think the nice things that have been said by fellow officials has meant an awful lot to me and the relationship that I've had with some of them I have really appreciated that an awful lot. I made a lot of friendships. They are certainly important to me and I think that they have been very important. I think they will be even more important in the years to come. I had a lot of wonderful things happen. I got the opportunity to work a lot of wonderful things.

"But I really don't think I was ever as good as I could have been. I wish very much that I had put even more effort into it and understood even better what it takes to reach the level that I wanted to reach. I would like very much to try to explain to other people that when they reach a certain level, regardless of what level or step they are working in, that's not the issue. The issue is they can be better but from their own it has to be from within. There ain't anybody going to hand them a book and say, 'You read this and that will take you to some other division.' It's got to come from the heart, it's got to come from the head, it's got to come from hard work with the body and you just have to do it, but it sure as heck is worth it. I would like very much to encourage other officials to push themselves harder."

3

Body Language
Speaks Volumes

By Bill Topp and Jeffrey Stern

JIM WHITE

Don Rusk,
Indiana

When people hear the word "communication," they think of how one person speaks to another. A sometimes overlooked yet critically important method is body language. In many ways, an official's body language is just as important as verbal communication. Just like profanity to a player or coach can get an official in trouble, poor body language can escalate a negative situation. Conversely, positive body language helps ease and control a potential conflict.

At all times, stand tall and firm. Use good posture. It will help give an appearance of confidence and possibly reduce the number of conflicts. Hold your head up; don't dip your chin.

When a player or coach challenges you, consider what your body language says to the arguer and the observers (other players, coaches, fans, etc.). Avoid crossing your arms in front of your chest. That movement appears too aggressive. Also avoid a strong looking "hands-on-hips" stance with your chest thrust out. Again, the official appears the aggressor. When an argument ensues, consider placing your hands behind your back. Stand tall and strong while doing so. That stance does not appear confrontational, yet shows you're in control. At all times, avoid pointing at a player or coach. Using that gesture appears too aggressive and almost always gets a heated response like, "Get your finger out of my face!" Make solid eye contact during the discussion. If your eyes wander or your head moves around looking elsewhere, it appears you're either intimidated by the coach or are not interested in what's being said. Neither is good for the conversation. Also, try hard not to scowl.

Make solid eye contact during the discussion.

From the moment you arrive at the game site, pretend there's a TV camera pointed directly at you. In effect, you're on stage.

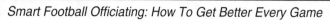

Think about what you would look like if you were on TV and there was no sound. Here's a situation in which body language affects a discussion with a coach:

In a game played under NFHS rules, it's second and 25 on team A's 30 yardline. As runner A1 gains three yards, he is pulled to the ground by his facemask. You penalize team B 15 yards and award an automatic first down. Team B's coach calls a timeout and requests a coach-referee conference to ask you about the call. Early in the exchange, the coach is calm and talking in relatively normal tones. The coach simply wants an explanation of the call, saying, "I know it's a 15-yard penalty, but I'm positive it's not an automatic first down. Is there a chance you're mistaken?"

While the coach is talking, you don't say anything verbally but your body language shows you're not thrilled with the coach. You fold your arms in front of your chest, have a smirk on your face and then roll your eyes when the coach says, "I'm positive it's not an automatic first down."

Watching your body language, the coach becomes agitated and says, "Hey, I'm just out here asking a question and I have a right to do that. I've shown you respect and expect the same from you." With that, you raise your hand as a stop signal, then wave the coach back to the bench as if dismissing him, all with a cocky smile on your face.

Instead of backing down, the coach then gets closer to you, stands firm and yells, "You've got an attitude problem! You're not bigger than the game. I'm going to send a report to the high school state office. This is ridiculous! Your attitude stinks!" You then flag the coach.

Through the whole scenario, you didn't say a single word. Yet your body language screamed at the coach a variety of things, including disrespect, cockiness and an unwillingness to listen.

Better body language — eye contact, comfortable stance with hands behind your back, maybe even a "yes" nod to let the coach know you understand the concern — coupled with a solid verbal explanation would have helped you address the coach professionally and avoid a heated argument.

Your whistle and your flag are communication tools. When you blow a weak whistle, you're more likely to be challenged because it sounds like you're not sure of yourself. Conversely, a constant, overly loud whistle equates to screaming. There are times when you need a loud whistle (to get a person's attention, in a loud setting, to help "sell" a call, etc.). But if you're constantly blowing your whistle as loud as you can, it would be like you're yelling every time you speak. Blow a strong, steady whistle with normal volume in most situations. Don't use short, repetitive blasts except to let the referee know a flag is on the field. Otherwise, short, repetitive blasts draw unnecessary attention to the official. Think of your whistle as an extension of your voice. Most of the time, "talk" with normal tone. If the situation requires you to be a bit louder and firm, blow your whistle a bit harder. Use that tone sparingly.

When you blow a weak whistle, you're more likely to be challenged.

The same principles apply to throwing a flag. The way you use your flag is a method of communicating. If the flag you throw looks more like it simply fell out of your pocket, it's a weak flag, suggesting that you're unsure about what you called. An "angry" flag occurs when an official gets emotional about a call. Slamming the flag into the ground also equates to screaming. It appears the official has lost control and is belittling the offender. Throw the flag with an arc so that it flies gracefully through the air toward the area of the foul. By doing that, it doesn't look like you're throwing aggressively at someone. Remember that while knowing the spot at which is a foul occurred is important, the offending player is not to be treated as a target. You can throw your flag to either side of the player without hitting the exact blade of grass representing the spot. Not only does that reduce the chance that a player may get injured by your flag, it looks less confrontational.

The way an official looks and the presence the official carries during the game goes a long way toward managing conflict. Simply put, you've got to look like you know what you're doing and look confident while handling situations. That includes physical presence.

Presence is a difficult thing to define. An official with presence is athletic-looking and has a confident demeanor that says, "I belong." An official without presence often looks nervous and appears to be anxious. Coaches can sense that and may become aggressive, thinking they can easily influence that official and can gain an advantage.

Age is a factor that you can't control. Younger officials should be prepared to deal with more conflict than an older official. Coaches tend to test rookies because there's a perception that they are more easily influenced than veterans. Realizing that, you can better prepare by thinking about what you are going to say before you say it.

Good officials look good. They are physically fit and appear athletic. They walk confidently with a strong posture. How does that relate to managing conflict? The better you look, the more accepting people are. The more accepting people are, the less conflict you'll have to manage. Your physical presence also means where you are in relation to the conflict. Sometimes you can defuse a situation merely by being in the area of the problem.

Here's an example. When two players (or more) end up on the ground due to aggressive playing action (such as a play that ends out of bounds), the covering official should immediately move toward the players. If the first person a player sees is an official in that area, there is less likelihood of retaliation (verbal or physical). If you aren't there, a player might try to get away with an intentional elbow or a push to the opponent.

Convincing a crowd your call is correct requires the fine-tuning of style: Using body language, facial expressions and sounds to sell your calls. An official's success depends not only upon accuracy but how well he convinces others his decision is correct.

Such seemingly insignificant variations as the duration and intensity of blowing a whistle, the speed and crispness used when giving signals or vocalizing calls play an important part in the determination of competency.

An official's success depends not only upon accuracy but how well he convinces others his decision is correct.

Appear hesitant when you throw a flag and fans may instantly doubt you. Offer a "soft whistle" on a dead-ball foul and your judgment may be questioned.

The trick is to maintain consistency in style. An official who suddenly behaves frantically communicates a temporary loss of control. An overly modest response suggests uncertainty.

Timeout for brief eye contact or a nod of the head communicate a sense of carefulness on the part of the officials. Quick responses are not the only acceptable way of working. More important is consistency of timing: Any sudden change in the rhythm of an official between the event and the signal is likely to be taken as an indication that something's amiss.

Consistency is maintained by delaying calls of the obvious happenings in order to match the time for those requiring reflection.

By the same token, the body language of players and coaches can tell you a great deal. You can't prevent a conflict if you don't recognize clues to volatile emotions. Some conflicts are easy to recognize; two opponents swinging fists at one another is a clear indication. You must learn how to recognize signs of conflict that you can deal with before a situation escalates. When you read the signs correctly, you can prevent major blow-ups from happening.

Frustrated players tend to complain or demonstrate non-verbal signs of disgust. Knowing the signs of frustration gives you the context to deal with the player appropriately.

Always watch for contact away from the ball or after a play ends.

A player's poor performance is an obvious sign of a player's frustration level. If a player is playing well, you're less likely to hear complaining. If a star player is struggling, you'll hear more complaining (it's part of being a "scapegoat").

Look at players' facial expressions and body language for clues about their behavior. Staring or glaring at an opponent is an obvious attempt at intimidation. Tense facial muscles, such as a set jaw, may indicate a player is close to acting aggressively. Also players who scold teammates are usually frustrated.

Always watch for contact away from the ball or after a play ends, including after scoring plays. Kick trys in particular are ripe for a cheap shot (verbal or physical) because of the perception that no one is watching.

Be constantly on the lookout for "paybacks." For example, at higher levels of competition, if a player committed a personal foul, look for the offended player to attempt to get the player back at some point. Not-so-smart players attempt to retaliate immediately; they are often caught because the officials are still focused on those players. Smarter players try to get away with retaliation a short time later, hoping the referees aren't watching anymore.

Most signs from coaches are verbal. When their comments to officials are repetitive, it is usually a sign of either "working" the officials or frustration. The volume of their comments is also a sign. Watch for impulsive, attack-style body language too.

Look for how they talk to their own players and assistant coaches. If they're haranguing them, the officials may also probably be a target at some point.

Body language is crucial. Look for stern facial expressions that express anger or a roll of the eyes and a wry smile that suggests sarcasm. A coach flailing arms or using officiating signals is a sure sign that the coach is playing to the crowd in an attempt to intimidate you.

4

The Four Cs
of Officiating

By George Demetriou

Mike Williams,
California

Several years ago, I had the privilege of hearing a coach speak at a meeting of our local association. Dom Luppino, who'd been at helm of the Liberty High School Lancers for more than 10 years, related what he expected of officials. He titled his talk, "The Three Cs." To be honest, I don't remember his exact words or the examples he used, but his message stuck with me, particularly the "Cs."

There are many words beginning with "C" that describe the qualities of a good official. Among them: character, confidence, creativity, credibility, courage, coverage and calm. I cannot possibly cover them all in this chapter. Instead, I've taken Dom's three selections and added one.

Consistency. This is perhaps the first word that comes to mind with respect to good officiating, even if you don't restrict yourself to "C" words. Consistency means several things. First of all, you must get all your calls right. If you do that, no one will accuse you of inconsistency. Eliminate any preconceived idea of how the game should be played. Take the game you get and do what you can with it; do not try to make it into something it is not.

Fairness is another issue. Frequently a no-call is appropriate. The same actions should result in the same call or non-call. Each call must be judged on its own merit and must adhere to the intent of the rules.

Now that I've discussed what consistency is, I'll say a few words about what consistency is not. Consistency is not calling the same number of fouls on each team. There are many who believe that and basketball officials hear it the most often since the fouls are posted for all to see. In a football game, the difference must be unusually large for it to be noticed. I had a game where the captain approached me at the end of the first quarter with just that complaint. My answer: "You've had the ball

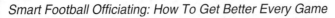

most of the time and more fouls are called on the offense than the defense."

Please bear in mind that you may not be able to change a particular coach's concept of consistency. I know an excellent official who has been blackballed at a local school for more than 10 years because the coach felt he raised his arms more vigorously to signal an opponent's touchdown than he did for the home team!

Caring. This one perhaps sounds odd. Officials are not usually thought of as caring people, nor do most people expect them to be caring. The stereotype simply doesn't call for such an approach. On the other hand, the number-one reason for being an official cited in surveys is "love of the game." If you love the game, why can't you love the kids who play it and the men who coach it (in a platonic sense, of course)?

Whether you're dealing with teenagers or young adults, you should not forget that is what they are. They'll make mistakes, they'll do stupid things and on occasion, they'll act their age.

I was the referee for a high school freshman game. As the quarterback dropped back, a rusher came in and tried an arm-tackle around the quarterback's waist. As the quarterback fell backward, the tackler's arm slid up his chest. The defender's forearm glanced off the quarterback's chin and then his facemask. It was simply a lousy tackle that happened to succeed. As the quarterback arose, he hotly inquired, "Aren't you going to call the facemask?" I replied, "He didn't grab it; he inadvertently hit it." Here was a kid who was upset at being sacked and the blow he took was salt in the wound. As he stomped back to the huddle, he turned and glared at me with a look that clearly implied, "Bulls—-." I merely replied, "Watch it," and turned away.

Now we come to the coach. The coach bears a burden players and officials do not. He has to stay on the scene and face the music, whether it be parents or administrators. Players graduate and you'll move on to another game, but the coach usually wants to stay. Your decisions are part of his history and he can be fired for losing, whether you were right or not. Is it any wonder then that coaches, from a parochial position to begin with, will question close judgment calls?

A few years ago, I worked a game with a good but hot-tempered official I'll call Tony. On one particular play, Tony threw his flag for holding. When the played ended, I saw Tony wagging his finger at the offender and giving him a royal dressing-down. At the half, I cautioned Tony, ending my advice with, "Coaches don't like that." His reply: "I don't give a hoot. All coaches are (expletive deleted)." I felt like asking him why he bothers to officiate.

Being a caring official won't show on the evaluation sheet. Your reward is inner satisfaction.

Being a caring official won't show on the evaluation sheet. Your reward is inner satisfaction. In the end, the only one you have to answer to is the guy in the mirror each morning. Make sure he is a credit to the game and a protector of player safety. Remember that it's OK to let the players know you're human.

Control. There are two keys to exercising control: preventive officiating and self-control. A problem prevented is a problem solved. Talk to the players early about marginal holding, being set for less than one second, etc.

Preventative officiating is not limited to verbiage. If necessary, flag marginal late hits early. In the semi-pro league I work, defenders have a penchant for taking a shot at quarterbacks. One step and a blow draws my flag where two steps and a legitimate tackle won't. It works; no one wants a second flag — even in a "blood" match.

There are limits. The amount of preventive officiating used can destroy as well as enhance the tempo of a game. This is the nebulous part of officiating. Each official must develop the ability to discern when he should prevent and when he should simply make the call. This ability to discriminate is one of the things that separates the great officials from the average ones.

Before you can control players and coaches, you must be able to control yourself. You must have poise at all times and you can't afford to get mad. During arguments, you must be patient and slow to anger. Once you lose your head you have lost, despite the fact you'll "win" the argument.

Exercising control should be distinguished from exerting power. Power is ego-centered, personalized and confrontational. If you don't take yourself seriously, you won't have trouble avoiding coming across as a power broker.

Communication. From the coaches' perspective, they need to know what's going on, are entitled to know and should know. The number of a player committing a foul should be relayed to the appropriate coach by the wing official on his sideline. On occasion the covering official won't get the offender's number. Don't guess. Many years ago, a member of the late Gene Calhoun's Big 10 crew tried to hang a personal foul on number 77 of Illinois. That happens to have been Red Grange's number and had been long retired. That crew's credibility went out the window.

Don't underestimate the value of clear and concise signals. A signal that is worth giving is one that is given as stated in the rulebook and can be seen. Give it out in the open, away from the players and after coming to a full stop.

For the officials to communicate with the coaches, there must be a good system of intra-crew communication. Supplementary signals are available for crew members to remind each other of several items. Included are two stakes to gain a first down, receivers on and off the line, don't start the clock, watch the snapper, next play kills the clock, etc. In many cases, those signals are unnecessary. Lung power works better. There is nothing wrong with talking to your crewmates during dead-ball periods.

When an unusual play occurs, take the time to explain the outcome to both coaches. On occasion, preemptive communication may be wise.

Let's say you're working a prep game and team A is driving for the winning score inside team B's 10 yardline with five seconds remaining. The offense holds and the defense accepts. After enforcement, the clock should be started. If you do that and team A does not get the snap off, team B and its fans will think the game is over. That's a case when an explanation of the untimed down rule is worth giving in advance.

Counter to the positive "Cs," are the negative "Cs." Among them: caustic, cocky, complacent, critical, cranky and confrontational. Which "Cs" do you follow?

5

Things We Never Fail to Do

By Jerry Grunska

ED PURCELL

Bob Brown,
Illinois

Oversight is an annoying thing, because the instant you realize you've forgotten or neglected something, the recognition brings acute regret, and there's no way to erase the feeling.

But sometimes we don't even recognize that we've fallen short. What's more, when someone brings it to our attention, we may become angry or defensive. Another way to deal with neglect is denial.

In an effort to prevent or offset all of the above reactions, high school crew chief Wayne Kendall of Mt. Prospect, Ill., a suburb of Chicago, drew up a list of behaviors that he drilled into crew members. He insisted that they not only memorize the items, but also instituted penalties if any of the specified behaviors were overlooked by a crew member during a game.

His foundation of performance paid off. Before long, Kendall's crew was selected to work a state playoff championship final.

One of the mandates Kendall formulated was that the clock would be stopped promptly on all clock-killing situations. To be sure, a rather standard undertaking. It was number-one on his list of "Things We Will Never Fail To Do." Easy for him to say, right? Here's how he went about assuring compliance.

• When a sideline official relayed the ball back to the hashmark after a play ended out of bounds, he had to tell crewmates, "I've killed the clock."

• If a play carried near the first-down stake, the line judge had to call either "short" or "I killed the clock; first down." A third vocalization was "Freeze it; we might have to measure," whereupon the referee decided whether or not a clock kill was necessary. The covering official also had to notify the ref if the clock were to be restarted.

• If the clock were to be kept alive on a close-to-sideline play, the covering official would have to say "I wound it" as he relayed the ball back toward the hash.

• After any fourth-down play or change of possession, the covering official was obliged to say "I killed it" before the referee would accept his version of the play's result and subsequent status of the clock. For example, after a possession change, the covering official was required to say, "Clock stays dead."

• Any explanation of a foul, to the referee, had to be preceded by the statement "I killed the clock." If the official started to recapitulate the foul, the referee would interrupt by asking if the clock had been killed.

• On any fumble that required "digging" by the officials, the first official arriving at the pile had to shout, "I killed it" before probing. Other arriving officials were to say "echo," meaning they had reflected the clock-kill with signals of their own. In fact, the crew emphasized clock-kill mimicking and made it a point to remind one another, the purpose being to make sure the clock operator was continually informed.

Before each fourth-down play, all officials used the phrase "clock stopper," followed by an unobtrusive hand signal, to remind each other about stopping the clock at the end of the down.

After a possession change, the covering official was required to say, "Clock stays dead."

Furthermore, whenever a crew member killed the clock, his next obligation was to check the game clock to see that it was halted. The referee constantly asked, "Have you checked the scoreboard?" after he got a clock-kill report, and he expected a curt, straightforward "yes" every time. Sometimes his mates would twit Kendall with a sardonic, "You betcha. You betcha! I have indeed terminated it." Spit-and-polish was a requisite, but it didn't have to be gruesomely formal.

Any crew in the football world could benefit just by focusing on strict clock-handling procedures. Desultory timing tactics are a shortcoming of prep level crews everywhere.

If you get the impression that Kendall's crew did a lot of talking while administering a game, that observation is correct. Lots of officials move through a game with jaws clamped on their whistles, and all habitual behavior is basically a pantomime. Then when something goes wrong because they haven't developed a routine of effective communication, they'll chastise themselves and say, "We have to talk more." A key thing about the aspects of verbalizing that are described here is that while repetitive they are not frivolous. Strong and ongoing communication can become just as habitual as dummying up. It just takes a conscious desire and practice. Practice will also help it become smooth.

Kendall also insisted on a patterned routine of voicing when he came downfield after a punt. He wanted the covering official, usually the back judge, to remain with the ball and tell him exactly what had happened. Some examples of the information proffered:

• "Runback, receivers' ball right here at the 36 yardline. I killed the clock and signaled the first down."

• "Attempted fair catch. Muff. Kickers recovered here at the 42 yardline. I killed the clock."

• "Fair catch signal by number 32, but teammate 24 caught the ball and ran. I killed the clock and dropped a bag at the reception spot." If necessary, the official would add, "I also flagged the receiver for delay."

• "Muffed fair catch. Kickers picked it up and ran with it, but I killed the play and the clock, and I bagged the spot of recovery."

• "Two first-touching spots by the kickers, one here at the 45 yardline and the other downfield at the 40 yardline, where the kickers downed the ball. I killed the clock, marking the first spot with one bag and the second with my backup beanbag. Receivers will take it here at their own 45 yardline. Clock starts with the snap."

Too much verbiage? Not if you want to get it right. Every time without fail. Not if you want to leave the mysteries and confusion to others. Not if you want to work a little harder to be sure whatever complexities arise, you'll be able to walk through them verbally, step-by-step, so that everybody understands perfectly what happened and how you ruled, including yourself.

Here's a play that could sound bizarre, but in truth it is plausible, and it demands real processing and instant reactions on the part of covering officials. If you can talk your way through it, you can officiate your way through it too.

A punt carries across midfield and lands at the receivers' 25 yardline. A player from the kicking team tries to stop it at the 20 yardline, but the ball bounces off his outstretched hand and is touched again by a kicking teammate at the 15 yardline. The ball wobbles to the 10 yardline, where a receiver picks it up and runs to his 30 yardline. He is hit there and fumbles. A player from the kicking team scoops it up and dashes to the end zone.

A score, right? Not really. The receivers get to take the ball at the spot of first touching, the 20 yardline. But should the covering official have killed the play when team K recovered the fumble at the 30 yardline? Should they signal touchdown when team K runs it across the goalline? No in both cases. The team K player could have fumbled himself before he got to the goal, and team R could have run it back for his own touchdown; therefore, no whistle. The ball stays live until the end zone is reached, and then the officials must tell the referee what happened.

Are they likely to garble their explanation? Will they stammer and shrug their shoulders in hapless puzzlement? Perhaps so, if they're not really used to explaining weird happenings at the end of punts. And any experienced official will affirm that weird things do often occur on punts.

But let's throw a monkey wrench into the ointment, to frazzle a phrase. Let's say that when team R picked up the punt at his own 10 yardline, after the double-touching by team K, while on his way out to fumble at the 30 yardline, one of the team R players committed a clipping foul. Now when the team K player chugs into the end zone he's got a touchdown, right?

"We've got a touchdown for the kickers because they ran back a fumble from the 30 yardline. Team K's first touching — see the two beanbags? — is ignored, due to team R's foul afterward, while in possession." If only your explanation could come out that clearly.

Another of Kendall's directives was, "We're going to count the players on every single play." By now you know that such a directive is standard operating procedure on all college and pro crews, plus they signal to one another. A simple fist held up at shoulder height or a "thumbs up" sign says we've got a full complement of players, no more, no less. If you count in bunches of three or four, it only takes two or three seconds to accomplish it. But it does take practice. You have to develop a rhythm.

Several points here. The defense can be counted while the offense is in its huddle. If the team is short players or has an extra player, the line judge and back judge should use a signal that says, "I've only got 10," or "Looks like a dozen to me." That way neither official will be confused to see a substitute come on the field at the last second or become startled to see the extra man leave. The defense is more vulnerable for an improper number of players, because it does not have set and eligible positions as the offense does.

Incidentally, it is especially critical for the defensive duo (meaning the line judge and back judge) to synchronize their counting on kick situations, because receiving team players are often streaming in or out, sometimes separated a considerable distance from each other. That is, a linebacker may dash to the sidelines while a deep receiver sprints onto the field in his place. A caution too: When the offense is running a "hurry-up" set of plays, it may be difficult for the line judge to help the back judge in his counting. Then the crew has to rely on a single individual to keep track of defenders.

In terms of correct numbers, the offense, on the other hand, usually recognizes shortages and overages, because players will spot vacancies or duplicates of their assigned position. No team is likely to put two snappers on the field at once, for example, nor a pair of quarterbacks. Backs and ends. They may be on opposites ends of the line and not be aware of each other. And that's what officials should look for. The advantage of having two "center field" officials (umpire and referee) count the offense is that they can then "read" the formation, much as defenders must do, to be aware of which play may be coming. The referee is usually the official who will flag a team for breaking the huddle with 12 players or for other offensive substitution infractions.

If you've ever played football, you know that assignments are given in the huddle when the play (or defense) is called. Players coming up to the line are making mental notes of their responsibilities and observing the proximity of opponents. No official has a right to intrude upon that concentration. Seriously, you have to know how people play the game.

How does a linesman know that the line-to-gain is being approached or passed on a given play? That is a tricky problem and solving it demands continual alertness, plus constant reminders. On Kendall's crew the linesman and line judge had a signal system worked out so that before each play they "told" each other how far the lead stake was from the scrimmage line.

As soon as the referee marked the ball ready, both wing officials pointed to the first down spot on the field and nodded agreement. "If the ball comes dead near that yardline on the next play, we're either going to have a first down or it'll be close" was the non-verbal message relayed to each other. If the offense had suffered a loss or a penalty on previous downs, the two wingmen flashed a "two stakes" sign to one another.

Such "talking," they found, was a sure-fire way to keep their heads in the game and to guard against lapses in concentration. "For instance," Kendall said, "when I'm with another crew, the referee will often remind the line judge to tell us when we're approaching the lead stake, and the judge invariably agrees to do it, enthusiastically. Yet when the game is ripping along he forgets, and he may move the ball from his own sideline in toward the hash, and then somebody calls out that he should have let the ball lie for a measurement. So the ball has to be pitched back out to him and the whole scene looks sloppy. You can have a fiasco on your hands if the line judge isn't on the ball about that first-down marker."

The crew members found a sure-fire way to keep their heads in the game and to guard against lapses in concentration.

Sure you can. And if the line judge is vacant, the linesman may be forced to look back over his shoulder to spot the stake. That's forbidden behavior. A dead-ball foul may occur right in front of him the instant he wheels his head around for a glimpse at the stake.

"What are the consequences on your crew for failure to comply?" Kendall was asked. The negligent partner buys "treats" afterward: sustenance, libations, garnishments, the works. It's a strong incentive to "do right" on the field. "Sometimes, of course," said Kendall, eyes twinkling, "the tab is shared by more than one person." That method of accountability is an illustration of how the crew concept can be superior to individual assigning and to shoving people around from one position to another. A signal system among officials, for counting players, designating formations, and reminding about ball position relative to the chains, takes time and effort to coordinate. You are not likely to be synchronized to those refinements if you only work the position periodically or if there's no incentive to go beyond merely running the game with little effort to extend yourself to create "cutting-edge" communication measures.

An observer questioned Kendall about his crew's doing things that the manual doesn't specify. "The manual can't possibly cover everything," Kendall said. "It describes the basics, naturally. We subscribe to them all. But we've added actions that fit the true elements of the game, helping us to be better administrators. They are simply extensions of what the basics imply. We're trying to be super-efficient. We want to make sure no stone is left unturned in methods of coverage and in ways to communicate that help us run the game successfully. We're determined to be the best!"

As moves toward that end, here are some more of the practices that Kendall's crew has made "routine." The word routine is put in quotes only because what may be customary for one particular crew may be unheard of by a great many other groups. Here's Kendall's precise explanation for attempted scoring kicks from placement. "Back judge and line judge under the bar; umpire moves slightly to the line judge's side; but actual responsibility for the sideline and goalline in the event of a fake or broken play falls on the referee, who must be very wide, on the line judge's 'open' side.

"Linesman squeezes in toward the center of the scrimmage line to help umpire unpile players after the play. Linesman also turns his head to observe the kicker/holder when the referee pivots to reflect the signals from the underneath duo. 'Yes-yes' or 'No-no' are the only words exchanged by the covering judges beneath the crossbar. No other creative terms are permitted. If the kick is wide to one side, that side official will add a 'selling' wave-off."

The impressive thing about the directive is its precision and utter simplicity. It is virtually impossible to misunderstand. Yet how many linesmen really help in scrimmage coverage after a play? How many look to the kicker/holder as a guardian for the referee? In fact, how many umpires stay with the line to supervise their unpiling after extra point kicks? Only a few. Once a kick sails across the endline, many officials simply turn and jog upfield, leaving 22 players to fend for themselves in the play's aftermath. A dangerous precedent.

Here are some other mantras that the crew followed to the letter:

• Know who has goalline responsibility and vocalize it. Point out the goalline every time it is a factor.

• All relay passes (underhand shovel tosses) will be no longer than 10 yards. Either official may shorten the distance by moving forward, and the thrower must aim for the sternum of the receiver.

• Don't describe fouls. Report the technical term for the violation: Not "He grabbed him," but "Number 54, red, holding, at the flag, live ball, I killed the clock." Another official stands over the flag to make sure it is not moved.

• All violations will be reported to the sideline, with the exact player number. That means that an "off" official, one who did not make the call, may have to be aggressive in securing the necessary information to inform the coach.

• Before awarding a touchdown, the covering official will momentarily observe the actions of other officials. And he will also turn and observe players on their "follow through" into the end zone or across a sideline or endline. A moment late is less damaging than a moment too soon. Officials will signal a touchdown only when straddling the goalline.

• All player and coaching complaints will be listened to and reported to the necessary official, most notably to the referee.

• The referee shall vocalize the down and distance with every ready-for-play. That's in the mechanics books, but only about 10 percent of officials follow the practice.

• At every timeout the umpire shall verify the remaining timeouts with every crew member. Crew members must acknowledge that verification, and wing officials will notify their respective sidelines of both teams' remaining timeouts.

"Looking good" counts for nada if we've gotten something wrong — a rule mix-up or a judgmental error.

• Any official may execute a "tip" signal for a pass or kick that's been touched, including grounded kicks beyond the line. The official must know who committed the tip.

• Crew members will always request a crew conference if in doubt about anything. Getting it right is more important than looking good. In truth, "looking good" counts for nada if we've gotten something wrong — a rule mix-up or a judgmental error. Crew members will always say what they saw, even if it differs from another's point of view. Also, crew members will be receptive to another's point of view which may differ from their own.

Here's where you separate the men from the meager. That last segment stems from the realm of philosophy into the province of psychology. How can you dictate another person's attitude? Well, you can if you're a pragmatic, analytic and charismatic leader. You can ensure all of those behaviors in your constituents by instilling pride of accomplishment, a warm spirit of togetherness.

It's not exactly brainwashing, but it is a form of indoctrination. It's how the military takes raw youths and turns them into a force of efficient, polished and unified strength.

Keep in mind that the absence of such dedication is not necessarily a lackadaisical way of operating. Instead, it may simply be a comfortable version of complacency, an approach that says, "We'll be at ease out there, chewing on our whistles, pretty much closed-mouthed, and we'll worry about complexities whenever they pop up."

Yo, the problem with such a laisez faire approach is that something is bound to happen which will stir up the calm surface waters. odds are, serenity will be intermittently shattered. The further you go into detail about working cooperatively, the better prepared you'll be when a game gets hectic. It wasn't happenstance that Kendall's crew was labeled top-notch.

6

Defeating Negativity

By Jeffrey Stern

ED PURCELL

Referee Sal Caccauello and
back judge Terry Stephenson,
Illinois

Have you ever run across someone who had the ability to sap all the energy, excitement and intensity out of people? Someone with vampire-like powers to actually suck good feelings from your body and replace them with cynicism, dread and apathy?

Suppose you meet the rest of your crew at the appointed place and get ready to carpool to the game. You're primed for it; it's the big game between two crosstown rivals or two teams vying for first place, and you've been waiting all week for the assignment. When you arrive at the meeting place, a crewmate is already there, and he's complaining about the pressure the game has brought him all week. He's sure he's going to miss a call and screw up the outcome, and anyway he doesn't see why the game is such a big deal in the first place.

It doesn't take long before you feel your excitement wane and even turn to apprehension. Eventually, unless you're able to snap out of it, you stop caring, you become burned out and officiating becomes a chore. That is the power of negativity.

Negativity is an attitude or trait that affects everyone at one time or another. Whether they realize it or not, officials come face-to-face with a great deal of negativity — their own, that of other officials or that of coaches and players.

Although negativity is a mindset — a pattern of persistent pessimism — and not a disease, it has many of the same characteristics as an ailment. There are a number of ways to "catch" a negative attitude, including but not limited to contracting it from an associate. Once "infected," negativity affects a person physically and mentally, causing work performance to suffer. Unlike the common cold, however, there is a cure for negativity beyond simply letting the illness run its course.

What are the symptoms of negativity? The most obvious signs are a short temper, an unwillingness to ask for or accept offers of help and blaming others for one's shortcomings. Officials who fail to share information with colleagues and those who refuse to adopt standard mechanics and procedures may also be affected by negativity.

Although every case is different and the solution for one person's situation won't work for everyone, here are some suggestions that will help you overcome negativity.

A little help from your friends. Officiating in a crew has many advantages. But if one official is affected by negativity, crew effectiveness suffers. Although a crew will likely be comprised of people with varying temperaments, personalities and other traits, it is crucial that all officials pull on the same end of the rope during games. If one or more crewmembers brings a negative attitude to a game, the others may not be strong enough to win that emotional tug-of-war.

Many times the problem is situational negativity. That occurs when a specific recent incident causes one official to adopt a negative attitude toward another official.

For example, imagine a crew in the locker room at halftime. The linesman turns to the referee and says, "That intentional grounding call you made was terrible! There was an eligible receiver in my area but you went ahead and made the call anyway. The coach on that sideline is ready to chew my head off!"

The natural reaction to criticism is to yell back, "It's my call and I made it. I don't need help from you," but that only inflames the situation and answers negativity with negativity.

Another referee might be inclined to answer, "If there was a receiver there and you didn't come and tell me, you made the mistake, not me." That's an example of blame-shifting, a common mistake among officials.

Conversely, if the referee in the example responded, "You're right. The play could have been handled better," he has created a win-win situation. The linesman understands his crew chief will listen to his concerns and the referee has been given a tip for self-improvement. While most people would rather learn without a confrontation, the referee made the best of a potentially bad situation.

By involving the rest of the crew, the referee can even expand the situation into a learning opportunity: "Phil is bringing up a good point. How do you guys think we should operate when that happens? Should we get together quickly and talk about it before we enforce the penalty? Should I simply look to you for a nod yes or a shake no? What can I do to prevent that from happening again?"

Former Pac-10 football referee Bill Richardson, now an NFL replay assistant, says asking crewmates for help is not a sign of weakness. "I have opened (a crew meeting) by admitting that I need help with the clock after administering penalties. On the field or in the locker room, I'll thank the official when he gives me the status of the clock. By admitting your weaknesses, you may loosen up other crewmates."

Even if the referee is convinced he made the correct call, he can address the linesman's comments in a non-combative way. "I'd like another look at it," or, "It's possible I'd have called it differently if I had a different angle," allows the referee to acknowledge the comment without accepting blame.

The Velvet Hammer approach. Sometimes the problem is a state of chronic hopelessness. An official who moans, "I'll never be good enough to break into college ball," may well not have the skills to advance but should still be encouraged to try to be the best official possible.

A crewmate can step in and help. By using examples of previous success, a helpful partner can address that negative attitude. "Remember that play at the goalline in last week's game? You were in great position, your timing was excellent and your signal was emphatic but not overboard. That proves what a good job you're capable of doing." Such positive reinforcement helps rebuild the official's self-esteem and helps overcome the negativity.

A peer can also help by relating a tip that has proved successful. An example involves an official who moans, "I hate working a game at Central High because the coach constantly gets on me about my pass interference calls." Obviously that official enters games involving Central High with a feeling of dread, a negative attitude that likely exacerbates the problem with the coach.

A helpful partner might point out a mechanic the unhappy partner could try. "I used to have the same trouble until I realized that Central likes to throw to the weak-side receiver when they line up with two wideouts on the tight end side of the formation. When I see that formation, that is my key to watch the weak-side receiver. I started to do a better job of officiating that play and it really helped me do a better job on pass situations."

Notice the partner did not criticize and did not order the other official to try the mechanic. The unhappy official may find that the tip won't work, but it will inspire him to experiment until a solution is found. If nothing else, it will (at least for one night) replace the official's apprehension toward working a Central game with anticipation and hope that the new mechanic might make him a better official.

Sometimes it takes more of a kick in the butt than a pat on the back to shake a fellow official's attitude. Richardson says crewmates sometimes need to be lectured. The key is to do it in private, rather than risking embarrassment in front of other officials, spectators, coaches or players.

"I use the 'velvet hammer' approach," Richardson says. "I do not want to offend, yet I want to get my point across. Prepare your remarks before you criticize. Think and be a good listener."

Criticism from assignors and supervisors must be acknowledged differently than that from other officials. Because those who observe and hire officials sometimes have a "my way or the highway" philosophy, it is easy for an official to go into a critique meeting with a negative attitude.

Richardson says the key is an open mind. "Listen to what the supervisor has to say. Listening is different from hearing," Richardson says. "Don't plan your response while he is still counseling you. Know when you are getting defensive and know when and if to defend yourself."

A sure-fire way to prevent negativity in yourself (and boost your image in the eyes of the supervisor) is to ask before you're told. A supervisor who hears, "What can I do to get better?" is going to feel he has an official worth hiring. Such an official shows he is easy to work with and is willing to accept criticism.

On the other hand, supervisors are not fond of officials who engage in the "Yeah, but" syndrome. If you disagree with the supervisor, it is better to ask, "That sounds like a good tip; can you explain why your way is better than mine?" rather than respond with, "Yeah, but I tried it that way once and I missed three calls in a row," or, "Yeah, but doing it my way, I've worked the playoffs the last two years. If it ain't broke, why should I fix it?"

> **"Listen to what the supervisor has to say. Listening is different from hearing."**

The Green-eyed Monster. Enjoy any success in officiating, and you'll soon be faced with jealousy. Because officials in effect compete for plum assignments such as championship games or postseason tournament contests, it is easy for less-successful officials to resent those whose resumes are more impressive.

Many officials have been accosted by a counterpart who sneers, "I've officiated twice as long as you have, but you get playoff games and I don't. I guess it's not what you know but who you know."

It is sometimes satisfying to answer such a complaint with a comment such as, "I get playoff games because I'm a better official than you." In some cases, it would also be true. But such a retort will only further infuriate the jealous official.

That sort of negativity is better addressed by enlightenment. Information can be shared in a way that engenders thought. "You're right that I know some influential people. I met them at the annual camp at Hometown College. Not only did I make some valuable connections, I picked up a lot of tips that helped my officiating. I highly recommend the camp. Would you like to know how you can get a brochure?"

Such a technique puts the ball in the accuser's court. If he chooses not to take you up on your offer, he has no one but himself to blame. Yet you have not extended the feud because the challenge has been couched in the form of a non-confrontational tip.

Dealing with players and coaches. Officials most often encounter negativity when dealing with players and coaches. There are no magic words or proven formulas to convince a furious coach that a judgment call was correct or that a rule was properly applied. But there are ways an official can make the best of a bad situation.

Correct body language is perhaps the easiest technique an official can employ. Albert Mehrabian, a communications researcher from UCLA, conducted a study that found that 55 percent of a person's message is conveyed through body language (facial expression, body lean, hand gestures, etc.). Thirty-eight percent of the message was conveyed through tone of voice and only seven percent through the words being spoken.

From an officiating standpoint, that means facing an angry coach with a relaxed stance, hands behind the back and making eye contact. Acting calm projects an air of confidence and decisiveness. Let the coach make his point without interruption. Once the coach stops talking or begins repeating his position, explain the decision or the rule calmly and briefly.

An effective technique is making the coach answer questions. That transforms the coach from a challenger into a responder.

Imagine a play on which the official working the defensive team's side of the field determines that a runner's knee was down before he fumbled the ball. As the official jogs back to the sideline after marking the spot, he is confronted by the angry coach.

"That's a terrible call," the coach yells.

"Coach, are you questioning my decision or my interpretation of the rule?" the official responds.

"I want to know why that's not a fumble," is the response.

"The runner's knee was on the ground before the ball popped loose. The ball becomes dead when the knee hits, so what happened after that doesn't matter. Does that explain my ruling?"

The coach is unlikely to walk away happy but he will be satisfied you understand the rule and saw what occurred.

Body language entails more than body lean and tone of voice. Slamming the penalty flag rather than tossing it, chomping on the whistle and using jabs rather than smooth signals are other officiating practices that project negativity. They are all to be avoided.

See yourself in any of those examples? Negativity is infectious. It's like a disease, and like a disease it can ravage your joy for officiating and leave you burned out, apathetic and lackadaisical.

The next time you feel the creeping effects of negativity, whether they come from your own doubts or from an infected partner or crewmate, step back and examine the roots of the problem. You may not like the answer, but accepting it is the first step toward eliminating negativity.